Hello, This Is Your Body Talking

OTHER BOOKS & AUDIO PROGRAMS BY LUCIA CAPACCHIONE

Drawing Your Stress Away: A Draw-It-Yourself Coloring Book (Swallow Press/Ohio University Press)

The Creative Journal: The Art of Finding Yourself, 35th Anniversary Edition (Swallow Press/Ohio University Press)

The Power of Your Other Hand (New Page/Career Press)

The Creative Journal for Teens (New Page/Career Press)

The Creative Journal for Children (Shambhala)

The Creative Journal for Parents (Shambhala)

Recovery of Your Inner Child (Simon & Schuster)

Visioning: Ten Steps to Designing the Life of Your Dreams (Tarcher/Putnam)

The Art of Emotional Healing (Shambhala)

The Inner Child Playbook (e-book, at LuciaC.com)

The Talent Workbook (e-book, at LuciaC.com)

The Wisdom of Your Other Hand (5 CDs, at LuciaC.com)

The Picture of Health (CD, at LuciaC.com)

The Sound of Feelings (CDs with Jessie Allen Cooper's music, at LuciaC.com)

Visioning® (Musical accompaniment for the Visioning® process, at LuciaC.com)

TO CONTACT LUCIA CAPACCHIONE:

Visit: www.LuciaC.com & www.visioningcoach.org
Call: (805) 546-1424
Email: LuciaCapa@aol.com
Write to Lucia Capacchione at P.O. Box 1355, Cambria, CA 93428

For information about Creative Journal Expressive Arts Certification training with
 Dr. Lucia Capacchione & Dr. Marsha Nelson: www.LuciaC.com—Professional Training

Hello, This Is Your Body Talking

A DRAW-IT-YOURSELF COLORING BOOK

The Creative Journal Approach

Lucia Capacchione, PhD, ATR, REAT

Swallow Press ✦ Ohio University Press

Athens

Swallow Press
An imprint of Ohio University Press, Athens, Ohio 45701
ohioswallow.com

Printed in the United States of America
Swallow Press / Ohio University Press books are printed on acid-free paper ♾ ™

27 26 25 24 23 22 21 20 19 18 17   5 4 3 2 1

Contents

Introduction   1

PART ONE—BODY JOURNEY   19
    Scribbling Your Heart Out   19

Your Body, Your Self   23
    Breathing Meditation   23
    Inner Journey   24

Charting Sensations and Feelings in the Body   26
    Body Mapping   26
    My Body Map   27
    Writing about My Body Map   28
    My Body Part   29
    This Is Your Body Talking   31
    Becoming the Picture of Health   36

PART TWO—SELF-CARE: HEALTH IS AN INSIDE JOB   39
    Taking Care of You   40
    Making Time for Me: A Self-Care Calendar   41

Self-Care   42
    Making Space for Me   42
    Setting Boundaries   44

**PART THREE—WHAT'S IN YOUR HEAD?
MEET YOUR INNER BULLY**   45
    Facing the Inner Bully   46

Owning Your Own Thoughts   54
    Telling the Truth   54

The Inner Bully Turned Outward   57
    The Healing Letter   58

PART FOUR—WITH A LITTLE HELP FROM MY FRIENDS   63
The Power of Supportive Relationships   63

The Power of Support Groups   64
    The Gift of Friendship   65
    My Support System   68

Support System Diagram   69
Gratitude Rules   71
Rainbow Heart Meditation   72

Centering through Mandala-Making   74
Mandala of a Healthy Lifestyle   75
Mandalas for Inner Wisdom   77

To Your Health   83
Recommended Reading & Listening   85
Body Diagrams   86

Introduction

Drawing Your Way to Health

This is a Draw-It-Yourself Coloring Book. There are no lines to color inside. No pictures to fill in. No ready-made patterns or designs to follow.

The drawings in this book will be yours alone.

If you've used coloring books before, if you *think* you can't draw, if you haven't made art since kindergarten, if you are an amateur or professional artist, this Draw-It-Yourself Coloring Book is for you.

Wake Up and Smell the Crayons

In this book, you'll be scribbling with crayons, doodling and drawing with colored markers, pens, and crayons. You'll be making stuff that looks like, yes, kindergarten art. There are no grades, no performance standards or external critiques. No one expects you to make Art with a capital A. You're making this art just for you, just like you did as a little kid. This spontaneous approach to art (and writing) has actually been researched and proven helpful for de-stressing. It has also been shown to reveal the innate wisdom hidden in our body and mind. More on that later.

Relax! This is a safe space.

A private place to be spontaneous, playful, and childlike.

A critic-free zone to express what's inside.

I invite you to return to early childhood, a time when your Inner Artist was still alive. Remember the smell of crayons? Peeling the paper off when the crayon wore down? Scribbling as hard as you wanted to? Exploring colors and shapes with fat markers? Think of all the big, bold things you could do with them. Do you recall drawing out your feelings and the experiences that were important to you? Well, here's your chance to do that again.

I know, I know. You're probably freaking out, thinking: *Me? Draw? Forget it! I'm not creative. I have no artistic ability.* I hear those phrases from workshop attendees all the time. Here's what else they tell me:

> *Mom threw my kindergarten art in the trash. My teacher told me I had no talent. My brother said boys don't do art—it's for sissies. My older sister told me: Art is a waste of time. Dad said, You can't make a living with art, so major in English and become a screenwriter. (That last one is what my Dad told me, but fortunately I didn't do what he said. I became an artist.)*

Does any of this sound familiar? Growing up, did anyone ever criticize you for making art or discourage you from doing it? If you are afraid to draw, then that is probably why. Someone told you that you shouldn't or couldn't, so you didn't.

We Are All Artists (Until We Learn Otherwise)

After a first career as a successful artist and designer of posters and greeting cards, I became an early childhood educator. As a Montessori-trained Head Start supervisor (twelve centers), a national consultant, and a college instructor of nursery school teachers, I observed hundreds of preschoolers. I saw children in inner-city classrooms, upper-middle-class Montessori schools, and our middle-income college lab school.

I never heard one preschooler ever say: *I can't draw* or *I don't have any talent*.

They were *way* too busy drawing, painting, sculpting, and making murals and other art projects.

If you are like most people, it was later on—probably after first grade—that you learned you couldn't or shouldn't make art. Or they gave you premade outlines to color in, as if you didn't have the imagination to create your own pictures. You may have just stopped making art altogether. Or maybe you turned to old-school coloring books to sidestep those negative beliefs you learned about "no talent" or "not being creative." The so-called "inability" to draw wasn't a problem. You just colored in the designs provided for you by someone else. In the process, your natural ability to express from the inside out got squelched.

In recent years, coloring books for adults have become the rage. You may have used them yourself. If coloring books get people off their electronic devices for a while, I say: Bravo! If coloring books put art materials into people's hands, that's great! If coloring books get folks using their hands for something other than texting and typing on a keyboard for a bit, Hurray! But there's so much more you can do with crayons and colored markers, and it's **waiting right around the corner on the following pages.**

Let's face it: If you can write, you can draw. Period.
And I'll be guiding you in drawing and writing your way to better health.

For the Artists among Us

If you *are* an artist, you're lucky. You somehow escaped this kind of criticism. You ignored negative comments, persevered, and continued making art. But you'll have other issues with this new coloring book. In fact, you may have somewhat of a handicap because you are used to making art that looks good, is appreciated, exhibited, or sold. In the Fine Arts (with capital letters), the focus is on the *product*. I know because I am a trained artist. In both art school and the college art department where I studied, our work was critiqued and graded. The goal was to produce a *product* to show and eventually to sell our work. Some artists get commissions or assignments from clients. Either way, we produce products. Our personal process is secondary to the result: a completed painting, drawing, sculpture, mural, or piece of work in whatever medium we work in. That is definitely *not* the case in this Draw-It-Yourself Coloring Book. In this approach, the *process* comes first. This is art in the service of health. Your health.

Spontaneous Drawing Saved My Life

At the time I discovered that art (and writing) could heal, I was doing commercial design and teaching Art for Teachers of Young Children at Santa Monica College. One summer I fell ill with a serious yet mysterious illness that doctors were unable to diagnose correctly or treat. As I sat in a sickbed feeling as if I were dying, my sketchbooks started morphing into journals. I began spontaneously doing childlike, primitive-looking art that was not intended for the eyes of others. What a totally foreign concept that was for me! This strange-looking art-from-the-inside-out was portraying my inner life, my nocturnal dreams and some visions of the future that were buried inside my heart. Without realizing it I was healing myself by finding out what my body and emotions were trying to tell me through art (and later, through writing).

As a trained professional, this kind of art was extremely strange and uncomfortable for me. It was like nothing I had ever made before. I felt as if I were writing in a foreign tongue. My journal art looked nothing like the art I got paid for. These doodlings were almost surrealistic and I didn't understand them. I thought scribbling my feelings out was really weird. It resembled the art of mental patients I had seen on a career day tour of the Veterans Administration art program when I was in school. Maybe I'm really losing it, I thought. At the same time, it was oddly liberating to let my insides out onto paper.

Scribbling, doodling, and drawing helped me shed tension, pain, and fear. Through spontaneous art and writing, I vented anger, gave voice to anxiety, expressed confusion, doubt, sadness, and grief. I felt better after I drew in my journal, so I kept on doing it. It became clear that I was getting messages and guidance from my own body and emotions. *Could there be healing power in drawing feelings and bodily sensations?* I wondered. Within a few months the answer came: I recovered (without medical intervention) from a condition that was later identified as being in the family of lupus. Better yet, I regained a level of health and vitality I had never known. I was thirty-five when this journey began and thirty-six when I found a new career as an art therapist.

August 13, 1973

August 13, 1973

Self-Care

I learned many things from that illness. Perhaps the most important lesson was that self-care is essential for physical and mental health. It sounds obvious, doesn't it? But it's not happening in the United States. Judging from the number of television commercials for fast-food chains, beer, and junk food along with pharmaceutical drugs (to fix the problems the other products caused), we are not a nation that knows about self-care. In this coloring book, you will design a healthy lifestyle based on taking good care of yourself. Self-care is not selfish, as some people mistakenly think. Staying healthy is socially responsible, financially efficient, and just feels good. It makes us happier and easier to be around. And we have more energy for work, service, life, and love. Only you know the healthiest lifestyle for you, if you are willing to do some "deep listening" to your body and emotions. The drawing and writing prompts in the Self-Care section will guide you in choosing and sticking with that path.

The Inner Bully: Everybody's Got One

The other big lesson I learned from that illness was how toxic our own self-judgment is. It can contribute to making us anxious, depressed, and ill. After a few months of journaling with my body and emotions, I went into therapy and was shown how to identify the Critic in my own head. Mine was a monster and it had been literally "making me sick." We all have this voice of self-judgment in our own heads working 24-7, putting us down, questioning our worth, and making us feel bad: tired, confused, powerless, and even dispirited. I call it the Inner Bully.

In the outer world, we are all aware of the outer bullying that goes on in our society. Cyber-bullying has become an epidemic among today's youth. But what about the Bully turned inward that lives in our own negative self-talk? It's there 24-7, causing stress that can lead to irritability, creative blocks, fatigue, indecision, and illness. Any health program that ignores the stress caused by self-judgment is missing the mark. As a therapist, I've observed how violent behavior, morbid thoughts, self-harm, chemical dependence, eating disorders, plastic surgery addiction, and suicide can result from Inner Bullying. I have also observed how self-judgment gets turned outward and leads to bullying others. Whether turned inward or outward, the Inner Bully can wreak havoc within and without, weakening or even destroying our relationships.

I'll help you set the Inner Bully's self-criticism aside long enough so that you can have fun drawing and writing your feelings out. You'll be using researched and time-tested techniques for dealing with the Inner Bully and removing blocks in your everyday life. You'll learn to identify and stand up to the Inner Bully and scrutinize its words, detecting its partial lies and outright falsehoods. You'll relax and get back to scribbling and doodling freely, the way you did as a little kid. You'll draw and write your way into feeling better, both physically and emotionally.

Emotions, Stress, and Your Body

When emotions and worries are not expressed and dealt with, they get stored in the body. My clinical observations and research for over forty years have been supported by hundreds of studies on this subject. **Emotions that get stuffed into the body cause trouble.** You already know this intuitively. Think of the common phrases we all use and hear every day:

- She gives me a *headache*.
- He's a pain in the *neck*.
- I had a lump in my *throat*.
- I'm carrying the weight of the world on my *shoulders*.
- She's *shouldering* too much responsibility
- I had butterflies in my *stomach*.
- My *stomach* was tied up in knots.
- He couldn't *stomach* what she said to him.
- This job's a pain in the *butt*.
- She has no *spine*.
- My *knees* turned to jelly.

The Color of Feelings

We all know that listening to and playing music brings up feelings and sets a mood. So does art-making, especially when color is used. Colors express emotions. When coloring in this book, just remember this: we also use color to describe physical and emotional states. We feel colors physically; they register in our bodies. We refer to colors as *warm* (red, orange and yellow) or *cool* (green, blue, and purple). Feelings come in many colors. We've all heard or used colorful common phrases that describe emotional states.

- He turned *white* as a sheet.
- She was *green* with envy.
- He was *red* with rage.
- She was *yellow* (cowardly).
- I was feeling *blue*.

No Rules for Color

When it comes to emotional expression, colors mean different things to different people. For one person, the color red may bring up painful experiences or difficult emotions. For someone else, red might convey happiness and vitality. Over and over again at my workshops for people of all ages, cultures, races, religions, and backgrounds I see this: color is very personal. Each of us expresses ourselves through color in highly individual ways. If you ever learned a system of color symbolism, please set it aside for now.

There are no right or wrong colors for feelings.
There are no lists of color symbolism to follow.
The colors you choose are the *right* colors for *you*.
Be real, be honest.
Choose the colors that best portray your mood or emotion.

Unpacking Stored Emotions

As mentioned earlier, when emotions and worries get stuffed into the body, they cause trouble. We don't want to feel them. It's too painful. So we file them away in our bodies. Stored emotions can contribute to chronic or acute pain and physical or mental distress. When emotions go underground, they hide out in specific body parts. Some people store emotions in their backs, others in their heads. Some stuff emotions into their internal organs, like the bladder or liver. Where do you tend to store your emotions? You'll learn to find out in part 1: Body Journey.

Chronic conditions can result when the body becomes a closet packed with unexpressed worries, fears, frustrations, anxiety, anger, grief, and more. These stuffed feelings yell at us through symptoms: pain, discomfort, irritability, or fatigue. We can medicate the symptoms away, or cover them up with alcohol and drugs. But if the cause is stuffed emotions, sooner or later we pay the price: chronic pain or acute illness.

If we don't *feel* our emotions, we can't *heal them*.
Stop, look, and listen.
The body is a storyteller.
If we are willing to stop and feel,
if we listen deeply to our neglected emotions,
they can tell us a lot.
Stored emotions can actually talk to us,
telling us specifically what is causing our pain,

**what we can do to help ourselves,
or whether we need to get help from others.**

Sometimes a body part will tell us to see a professional (a doctor or masseuse, an acupuncturist or chiropractor). Other times our body may tell us to get more sleep, eat less sugar, get more exercise, stay away from negative people, get our feelings off our chest, change jobs, move to a different area, reach out to friends or loved ones. It may demand that we deal with our Inner Bully. This is some of the wise guidance you are likely to hear from your very own body. Part 1 contains prompts for feeling and listening to your body and to yourself. Let your body tell its story.

Art: The Language of Feelings

In this book we listen to ourselves using the language of feelings: art. We literally map out the body and color in the painful and uncomfortable areas where emotions are stuffed. Once we draw them, we can start feeling and accepting our feelings as being normal and natural.

**We literally draw emotions out of our body.
We also draw stressful thoughts out of our mind.**

The techniques used here are based on art therapy principles and my therapeutic writing methods.

What Is Art Therapy?

Art therapy is a form of psychotherapy in which a professionally trained therapist guides clients to express feelings, challenges, nocturnal dreams, and heartfelt wishes through spontaneous art-making. Clients are gently guided through age-appropriate activities (drawing, painting, sculpting, collage, assemblage, and more) using a broad range of simple art materials. Through art exploration, clients discover insights and inner resources they may not have known they had.

Art therapists, like all psychotherapists, are trained and credentialed professionals. Art therapy has been a recognized profession for over five decades. In the United States, we have the American Art Therapy Association (AATA), and other countries have their own art therapy organizations for professional credentialing. Hundreds of research studies on the effectiveness of art therapy have been published in professional journals. Art therapy has proven effective for addressing a broad range of issues, such as stress, life crises, trauma, marital issues, physical and mental illness (cancer, Alzheimer's), and more.

The art created in art therapy sessions is highly personal and kept confidential between the art therapist and the client. It is never intended as Fine Art for display or sale. There are no critiques. There is no pressure to make Art that is esthetically pleasing to anyone. This is process-oriented art in the service of mental and physical health, not for performance. Being a client in art therapy does not require any special talent or previous training or experience in art. Artists and other arts professionals also benefit from art therapy, as it provides a pressure-free zone for venting strong feelings, exploring the inner life and expressing bottled up emotions freely from the inside out.

Individuals of all ages, families and groups are being served by art therapists throughout the world. This approach to therapy has proven invaluable with preverbal children, adolescents, and adults of all ages and stages of life. Art therapy gives a voice to those who have not been able to express through words (young children, individuals on the autism spectrum, stroke patients, trauma survivors). Art therapy has proven effective for treating veterans with posttraumatic stress, those suffering psychological impacts due to physical injuries, cancer patients, and persons with AIDS/HIV.

The old saying,
A *picture is worth a thousand words,*
is absolutely true when it comes to art therapy.

Art therapy is also effective for clients with good, or even excellent, language skills. These clients often use speech to distract themselves from feeling uncomfortable emotions. They tend to stay in their heads (left brain language centers), analyze, rationalize, and second-guess themselves. This can result in confusion about how they *really* feel. Highly verbal clients also avoid feeling physical sensations, stay disconnected from their bodies, stuff their feelings, and become physically ill, fatigued, depressed, or even suicidal. Physicians and healthcare professionals have referred such clients to me when they can find no medically diagnosable condition for a patient's pain and suffering. Art heals.

Becoming an art therapist requires a postgraduate degree, followed by clinical supervision of work with clients. This is followed with certification by a qualified professional organization. In addition to AATA, there is the International Expressive Arts Therapy Association (IEATA), which encompasses all the arts therapies (art, dance, music, poetry, drama, photography, journaling, writing, and more). It covers all countries. I am a registered professional with both organizations.

Art Therapy = Process and Healing

Fine Art = Product and Exhibition

Coloring Books Are NOT Art Therapy

The term *art therapist* refers to a trained, credentialed professional guiding clients or groups through art therapy processes. One cannot simply call something art therapy. It's unethical to do so. Many popular adult coloring books claim to be art therapy. This is a false claim. Coloring in a traditional coloring book might be therapeutic, just like gardening or hiking may be therapeutic. But that doesn't make it art therapy. Neither is this book art therapy (although it is based on art therapy principles). Predesigned coloring books for adults may help some users feel calm and focused. That is a good thing. Coloring book enthusiasts report that coloring gets them away from excessive use of electronic devices and social media. This is a step in the right direction, but it's still not art therapy.

The approach in old-school coloring books is totally different from the spontaneous art done in art therapy. The whole point of art therapy is for clients to experience emotional expression from deep within themselves without external standards, judgment, or pressure to perform or to produce art for display. Clients get in touch with their inner life, finding insights and wisdom within. Art therapists do not give predesigned pictures or patterns to clients. There may be exceptions to this for a specific purpose, but they are exceptions. Giving clients premade designs contradicts the purpose of this form of art psychotherapy: free emotional expression from the inside out.

Coloring without Lines

So, let's color beyond lines.
In fact, let's get rid of lines altogether.
I invite you to
drop the "training wheels" on your creative expression,
so you can be free and fly.
As I often say:
"If you want to think outside the box, stop coloring inside the lines."

This is as true of life as it is of coloring books. If you want a handmade, original, authentic life, you came to the right place. If you want to get past your Inner Critic (I call it the Inner Bully) who demands perfection and wants you to color inside other people's lines (in life and in coloring books), *this* is the book for you.

Creative Journal Writing

The Creative Journal Method, which I originated in the mid-1970s, features drawing and writing in a journal. See my book *The Creative Journal* (Swallow Press/Ohio University Press). Here you will be using my method in a new format: the Draw-It-Yourself Coloring Book. In my method we usually draw first and then write *about* the drawing or write a dialogue *with* the drawing. Sometimes we simply let the drawing *talk to us* through the written word. Much of the drawing and the writing is done with the nondominant hand. I define that as the hand you don't normally write with. You'll be dialoguing with elements in your drawings, with body parts and with feelings. The dominant hand speaks for us (in our role as the interviewer). The nondominant hand gives voice to elements portrayed in the drawings.

The Healing Power of Your Other Hand

I'm naturally right-handed and stumbled into the healing power of my "other hand" while healing from that life-threatening disease I mentioned earlier. I have shared this technique of drawing and writing with the nondominant hand with thousands all over the world. The results are almost always the same. People tap directly into functions normally associated with the right hemisphere of the brain: improved visual-spatial perception, artistic abilities, emotional expressiveness, intuition, and creativity. After I started teaching these techniques, I discovered leading-edge research by brain scientists like the late Roger Sperry of Cal Tech (Nobel Prize, 1981) and Andrew Newberg (*Why God Won't Go Away*). Their discoveries supported my personal experiences and clinical research.

From the scientists, I learned that disease or injury to certain regions of the right brain impairs visual-spatial perception and emotional expressiveness. The right brain controls the left side of the body. By contrast, we know that the left hemisphere processes verbal, mathematical, and logical information. It governs the ability to follow rules of grammar, spelling, and syntax. Injury, stroke, or disease in certain parts of the left brain impairs speech and language functions as well as linear thinking and sense of time. The left brain controls the right side of the body.

Brain Functions of the Two Hemispheres

Right

Holistic

Sees the big picture

In the moment

Timeless

Feeling

Expressive

Musical

Artistic

Visual perception

Creative

Emotionally expressive

Sensory awareness

Esthetic arrangement

Body connection

Physical sensing

Spatial perception

Dreaming

Sense of rhythm

Intuitive

Creative problem-solving

Spiritual experience

Left

Order

Organization

Time-based

Reading

Writing

Syntax

Grammar

Speech

Math

Reasoning

Goal orientation

Analysis

Sequential logic

Numbering

Categorizing

Linear thought

Makes "to do" lists

Schedules

R L

Corpus Callosum

The corpus callosum is a bundle of nerve fibers connecting the two hemispheres of the brain. This enables the two sides to communicate. Writing with the nondominant hand has been shown to strengthen this connection. Activities in this book help you "let your left brain know what your right brain feels and needs."

The Brain at School

Our school systems generally teach to the left brain (the three Rs: reading, writing, and arithmetic). Science, technology, engineering, and math (STEM) programs are prized and get funding. The arts, which nurture right brain skills, are neglected and underfunded in most schools. We are educating only one half of the brain. Social, emotional, creative, and intuitive learning have become the stepchildren of formal education. This leads to *social-emotional and creative illiteracy.* What happens to feelings, empathy, and compassion? What about skills in communicating effectively with others? No wonder bullying has become an epidemic! What good are the three Rs if one cannot feel or speak the language of emotions? If one is left emotionally and socially illiterate and stunted? And installing classes called "Empathy" taught through left brain delivery systems will never do.

Research has been done in two public school districts (K–6): the Garvey School District in Southern California (1981–82), and the Edinburg Consolidated Independent School District in Texas (2014). Application of my methods in the classroom resulted in academic gains as well as behavioral and physical health improvements. This work in the schools has been documented in my books *The Creative Journal: The Art of Finding Yourself, 35th Anniversary Edition* (2015) and *The Creative Journal for Children: A Guide for Parents, Teachers, and Counselors* (1989). See the Mission Project documentary on YouTube: https://www.youtube.com /watch?v=s-8EZL-Kn8Y.

Why Write with the Nondominant Hand?

Because the left brain controls the right side of the body, it's no surprise that most people (about 85 percent) write with their right hand, the hand that is governed by the left (logical, verbal) side of the brain. Some people who write with their right hand are actually "switch-overs." Naturally left-handed, they were forced by parents or teachers to join the majority and use what was called the "right" (correct) hand for writing. This is not as common as it was when I started my practice in 1976, as schools tend to be more accepting of left-handers. However, it is something to be aware of. Using my methods, these "switch-overs" often uncover buried memories of being coerced into becoming right-handed for purposes of writing. In my clinical observations, many of these clients suffered neurological and psychological damage, developing learning disabilities or emotional problems after being forcibly switched over. Some of these clients have uncovered memories of the moment when they were forced to switch handedness for writing. Buried rage often pours out and an awareness that "something changed" in them for the worse. If that happened to you, I recommend my book *The Power of Your Other Hand.* In chapter 7 a "switch-over" tells his story.

What about Left-Handed People?

My observations show that left-handed people get the same results as right-handers when they use their nondominant (nonwriting) hand. They also access deeper levels of creativity, intuition, and emotional expressiveness (functions in which the right brain specializes). Science doesn't have an explanation for this yet, but I have volumes of data supporting this fact based on my over forty years of clinical experience and observation of thousands of individuals of all ages at workshops. For more about brain hemisphere functions, please see the TED talk online featuring Dr. Jill Bolte Taylor, author of *My Stroke of Insight*. Dr. Taylor (herself a brain scientist) describes the stroke in her left hemisphere which threw her into *right brain land*. Fortunately she recovered and shares her fascinating journey with the world.

The Write Way to Heal

A decade after I discovered the power of writing with the nondominant hand, I learned about a pioneering researcher in therapeutic writing: psychologist James W. Pennebaker. In a control-group study at Southern Methodist University in Dallas, Texas, the experimental group was asked to write about traumatic or difficult experiences, while the control group wrote about trivia. Blood samples were taken before and after the writing experiment and again six weeks later. Those who wrote about traumatic or difficult experiences showed an increase in lymphocyte response, which indicates an enhanced ability to fight infection. The control group showed no such strengthening of the immune system. Furthermore, the group who wrote about traumatic experiences made far fewer visits to the doctor in the six-month period following the experiment. Pennebaker's work laid the foundation for those of us who pioneered the new fields of journal therapy and writing therapy. After I met with him and shared my research, he was kind enough to endorse my book about writing with the "other hand." He encouraged me to continue my research into the healing power of *drawing* one's feelings out.

Sometimes Art Happens: If the Inner Artist Comes Out

After you start drawing in this book, you may be moved to use larger paper. If so, consider getting a spiral-bound sketchbook or hardbound sketcher's diary at an art and crafts shop, bookstore, or office supply store. Some of my clients and workshop participants go on to use oil pastels and even chalk pastels. If you use oil or chalk pastels, you'll need to spray the pages with hairspray or fixative so the oil or chalk won't rub off. Just remember, we are NOT trying to make Art with a capital A in this book. These drawings are *from* your Inner Child and are *for you alone*. They are not intended to "look pretty," please others, or meet aesthetic standards. You wouldn't expect a kindergartner to produce fine art, so don't expect it of your Inner Child. Just have fun.

Many of my readers write to me that artistic talent came gushing out unexpectedly after they used my Creative Journal Method. They tell me they had stopped drawing and painting when their early attempts at art were criticized harshly. How sad! But they feel liberated when they rediscover the artist within. It's never too late to find your Inner Artist. Think of famed landscape artist Grandma Moses, who started painting at age seventy-eight. If you do discover an interest or talent in art, by all means pursue it. Take some art classes or workshops. Do some art on your own. Just don't confuse the art done in this book with Fine Art that involves technique and finished products for display.

New Rules for the New Coloring Book

No external standards, no right or wrong.
Nothing to prove or accomplish.
(Wow!!! That makes me more relaxed just thinking about it.)
No one to please.
(These drawings are for your eyes only.)
There's no right or wrong way to draw in this book.
(You can't possibly make a mistake.)
No one will critique your work.
(The only goal here is to draw your stress out onto the paper.)
The only critic you have to deal with is the one in your own head.
(And I'll show you how to overcome that.)

Guidelines

1. Do activities **in the order given** when you use this book for the first time. If you re-peat activities, choose the one that best meets your needs at the time. You can repeat these activities on loose paper or in a sketchbook.

2. Keep your Draw-It-Yourself Coloring Book **private and confidential**. You do not need to risk negative comments or criticism from others. Keep it in **a safe, private place** to ensure confidentiality. We're learning to tame the Inner Critic, so we don't need or want any criticism from outside.

3. **If you wish to share, be selective.** Share your Draw-It-Yourself Coloring Book only with people you trust, who are not critical of you or what you are doing, such as loved ones, therapists, or counselors. Be selective about what you share. Explain to them that this information is private and confidential and not to be passed on to others.

4. Honesty is the key. If you can't be honest with yourself, then you won't benefit from these techniques. That's why it's important to keep it confidential. If you're worried about what others will think, you'll edit yourself and not be honest.

5. A **quiet, private place** is best when using your Draw-It-Yourself Coloring Book.

Note: If you are a survivor of childhood abuse, have been diagnosed with posttraumatic stress disorder, or have a history of psychiatric disorders or treatment, it is advised that you use this Draw-It-Yourself Coloring Book with the guidance of a licensed mental health professional.

Materials

1. *Hello, This Is Your Body Talking: A Draw-It-Yourself Coloring Book*

2. Art materials

   - Colored markers (wide tip for drawing) in twelve or more assorted colors
   - A set of fine-point pens in assorted colors
   - Crayons in assorted colors

   Note: I do not recommend colored pencils, as I find they are not as effective for releasing emotions as crayons, markers, and pens. People tend to get too detailed and pictorial with colored pencils and forget about the purpose of drawing their stress out on paper. When strong emotions are being released, pencil lead easily breaks.

3. Unlined blank book or blank white paper, 8½ x 11 inches

   If you find there is not enough blank paper in this *Draw-It-Yourself Coloring Book*, consider getting one of the following:

   - Blank book (hardbound or paperback with unlined pages)
   - Spiral-bound sketchpad with unlined paper
   - Three-ring loose-leaf binder with unlined paper

Preparing to Use Your Draw-It-Yourself Coloring Book

No matter which activities you are on, it's a good idea to begin with a few slow deep breaths or one of your own favorite relaxation techniques. Relaxation breathing is restful and healing. It regenerates the body and mind and opens up awareness, intuition, and creativity. Be sure that the place you've chosen is private, comfortable, and free from distractions.

**Creative Draw-It-Yourself Coloring Book time
is your time to be alone with yourself.**

Don't let anyone or anything encroach upon this very special time with yourself. For some, taking "alone time" may be difficult to do at first. Look at it this way: NOT taking time out *just for yourself* can contribute to illness and stress. So the first step toward feeling better is giving yourself this time. You deserve it!

Now you are ready to begin. Enjoy expressing your true self.

Part One

Body Journey

SCRIBBLING YOUR HEART OUT

Relax and enjoy making marks on paper without expectations; explore colors through scribbling; open up your right brain through drawing with your nondominant hand.

Materials: Colored pens, markers, crayons.

SCRIBBLING YOUR HEART OUT—1

Use your **dominant hand** (the one you normally write with). Choose colors that feel good to you by following your instincts. Make marks, doodles, scribbles, or shapes on paper. No pictures, symbols, or anything representational. No words. Start here in the blank space and continue on the next page.

Use your **nondominant hand** (the one you do *not* normally write with). Continue scribbling, doodling, and making marks on the paper. Remember, it's OK to feel awkward and childlike.

It's time to stop, look, and listen to your body sensations. As you become more aware of what is going on inside your body, you'll be able to catch symptoms of stress before they develop into full-blown illness. As you become fluent in the language your body speaks—nonverbal feelings and sensations—you'll get to the emotional roots of chronic ailments. The activities in this section are on audio: *The Picture of Health* CD (with my voice narrating and a relaxing musical background), available only at **www.luciac.com**. You can also record these meditations and play them back while doing the activities.

BREATHING MEDITATION

This is an exercise in breathing to be done in a quiet, private place. No distractions, no interruptions. Allow this very special time just for yourself. In order to relax and breathe fully, it is important that your spine be straight. So I'm going to give you simple directions for a reclining posture that will help you relax.

Lie on your back on a carpeted floor, yoga mat, or firm bed. Your legs are straight and slightly separated. Feet are twelve to eighteen inches apart. Your arms are at your sides about a foot away from your body. The palms of your hands are facing upward. Your chin is tipped slightly down toward the chest to elongate the neck. The back of your head is resting comfortably on the floor of the bed. (This is the Shivasana pose in Hatha Yoga.) If you prefer sitting in a chair, get as comfortable as you can. Do not cross your arms or legs. Your back needs to be straight and your arms resting in a comfortable position. Your feet are on the floor or resting on a solid surface.

Close your eyes and relax your body and mind. Focus your attention on your breathing. As you inhale and exhale, listen to the sound of your breath. Notice *how* you are breathing. Are you breathing through your nose or your mouth? Be aware of the rhythm of your breathing. Is it fast or slow? Observe *where* you take the breath into your body. Do you breathe high into your upper chest or lower down into your abdomen? How *much* air do you take in? Is your breathing shallow or deep?

Now relax and breathe through your nose. Inhale and exhale in a smooth and effortless rhythm. As you inhale, feel the air nourish and refresh your entire body. As you exhale, let the breath carry away tension and worry. Gradually allow your breathing to become deeper and slower. Don't force the breathing. Just allow the air to come in and go out in a steady flow. Slowly let your chest and abdomen expand as you fill up with air. Then release the breath naturally, letting go more and more. Relax into your body and the natural rhythm of your breathing. Feel how relaxed you are.

Now you will take a long, leisurely inner journey through your body. Close your eyes and take this trip slowly. Remain lying down comfortably on your back (or in your chair) as you practiced in the breathing exercise. As you go on your inner journey, pay attention to everything you feel inside. Imagine that your consciousness is shrinking down to a tiny point at the top of your head. You might see it as a tiny flashlight or a miniature hand. You are going to travel inside and feel the sensations in each area of your body.

Start at your forehead. Feel the sensations in this area. Do you experience tension or do you feel relaxed? Observe how your forehead feels. Then *slowly* move down your face. Check out the sensations around and behind your eyes. First your left eye, then your right. Do you feel strain or fatigue there? Or are you relaxed? Then move to your nose, cheeks, and sinus area. Observe the sensations there. Are you breathing openly? Or are you congested? Now slowly move down to your mouth, your chin and jaw. How does this area feel? Is it tense or relaxed? Go inside your mouth and check out the sensations in your tongue, gums, teeth, and other areas there. How does it feel?

Now move up to your ears. Check the sensations in and around your ears, first your left ear and then your right. Then go around the back of your head and gradually move up to the crown. Be aware of any feelings there. Then travel around inside your brain, first the left side and then the right. How do these parts feel? Observe all the sensations there.

Next, travel slowly down through your head to the inside of your throat. How does it feel there? Is your throat open or is it constricted? Does it feel good or is it sore? Check out your neck, both the front and the back. Is it tense or relaxed? Observe all the sensations there. Next, observe the feelings in your shoulders and the joints that connect your arms to your body. Be aware of the left shoulder joint and then the right. How do they feel?

Travel slowly down your arms; one arm and then the other. First observe the feeling in your left arm. Start with the upper arm, and then move down to the elbow. How do these areas feel? Then notice the sensations in your left forearm and wrist. Be aware of your left hand. Check out the palm, the back, and then each finger of your hand. How do they feel? Then repeat the journey, this time traveling down your right arm. Again start with the upper arm, moving down to the elbow. Notice all the sensations as your awareness moves from one area to the other. Observe the feelings in your right forearm and wrist. Then notice the sensations in your right hand: the palm, the back, and each finger.

Return to your torso. Move slowly down the front. Observe the feelings in your chest, heart, and lungs. Is this area tight and held in? Is it open and expansive? Do you inhale easily and deeply and exhale as naturally? Or do you experience constriction and difficulty in breathing fully? Travel next to your digestive system and through your stomach. How does it feel there? Move down to your bladder and internal organs. Move down to your intestinal area. If you feel sensations inside but are not sure which organ is causing them, simply note the sensations and the location. What kinds of feelings are you picking up in these areas? Next, move down to your genitals. Experience any sensations you are feeling in this area of your body.

Now, return to the back of your neck and observe the feelings in your upper back and shoulders. Is there tension and soreness there? Or do you feel loose and relaxed? Move slowly down your spine, down the middle of your back. Then observe feelings in your lower back and pelvic area. Is there any stiffness or soreness? Do you feel comfortable and relaxed? Continue down to the base of your spine, your anus, and buttocks. What kinds of sensations do you experience there?

Finally, move down your legs. Begin with the left pelvic joint and travel down your left leg. Observe the sensations in your left thigh. Then move down to your left knee. Are these areas tense or relaxed? Move gradually down the calf. Then check out all the sensations in your ankle. Lastly, move down into your left foot: the top, the sole, and then each toe. How does the foot feel? Now, repeating this journey, move your awareness gradually down your right leg. Start with the right pelvic joint and check out the sensations in your right thigh. Then move down to the knee. How does this area feel? Then move down your right calf to the ankle. Then check out your right foot: the top, the sole, and then each toe. What sensations do you feel there?

Relax fully and do a quick review of this inner journey. Make a mental note of any areas of stress, pain, or discomfort. When you inhale, consciously send the breath to those areas of your body. Take plenty of time. In this way you are nourishing the parts of your body that need tender, loving care.

Charting Sensations and Feelings in the Body

BODY MAPPING

Locate sensations and feelings in your body; learn to become more sensitive to your whole body.

Materials: Colored pens and markers.

Do the Breathing Meditation and Inner Journey.

Review the sensations you felt as you did the Inner Journey meditation. Locate the areas where you felt strong sensations: tensions, pain, soreness, irritation, pleasure, or relaxation. Let yourself really feel the physical sensations in your body.

Dominant hand. Draw an outline of your body on the next page.

Nondominant hand. Color in the areas where you feel sensations. Use colors, textures, shapes, and lines to express those sensations. *Note: There are body outlines (front, back, and sides) at the back of this book. Photocopy them for future use when you want to save time in doing this activity.*

MY BODY MAP

WRITING ABOUT MY BODY MAP

Materials: Your drawing from the Body Mapping exercise, colored pens.

Nondominant hand. Write the names of sensations and feelings in or around your body map.

MY BODY PART

Materials: Your Body Map drawing, colored pens, markers.

Choose the body part in which you felt the strongest sensations during the Inner Journey and Body Mapping activities. (If there were many such body parts, you can repeat this activity another day. If those body parts still need attention, you can follow the same guidelines. For now, choose just one body part.)

Nondominant hand. Draw a picture of that one body part that had the strongest sensations. If it's an internal organ and you are not sure what it looks like, simply follow your intuition. It does not have to be anatomically correct.

MY BODY PART

30

Verbalize physical sensations and emotions; use therapeutic writing for body awareness and well-being; communicate with your body and feelings.

Materials: Your Body Map, colored pens.

Dominant/Nondominant hands. Choose the body part in which you felt the strongest sensations during the Inner Journey and Body Mapping activities. (If there were many body parts, you can repeat this activity another day. If those body parts still need attention, you can follow the same guidelines. For now, choose just one body part.)

Interview the body part using the questions listed below. Write the questions with your **dominant hand**; let the body part answer with your **nondominant hand.** Use a different color pen in each hand. Don't preplan the dialogue. Let it happen spontaneously. Don't worry about spelling, grammar, syntax, or vocabulary. The nondominant hand often speaks and writes a language of its own, disregarding rules and conventions. It may misspell words, create new ones, or make puns. Your nondominant handwriting may be awkward, slow, and barely legible at first. As you get through the initial frustration it will get easier.

Four Healing Questions

- What are you?
- How do you feel?
- Why do you feel this way?
- What do you want me to do for you? How can I help you?
- Optional: What are you here to teach me? What is the lesson here? (This often gets answered with the first four responses. If not, then ask this question as well.)

What are you?
Stiff neck + head heaviness
left side
Why do you feel this way?
too many to do lists, too much
left brain stuff to do + keep
track of. It weighs me down.
Feels lopsided, carrying too
much. Need more breaks.

MY BODY TALKING

33

BECOMING THE PICTURE OF HEALTH

Create the image of how you want your body to feel; write positive affirmations.

Materials: Your Body Map, colored pens, markers, crayons.

Nondominant hand. On the next three pages, create a new drawing of your body that shows how you would like it to feel. As you draw, imagine the feelings of health and vitality associated with your new picture. Label this picture "Health."

In and around the drawing, create "word balloons" like those shown in comic strips. In each balloon, allow your Picture of Health to speak about how it feels. Examples: "feeling good," "standing up for myself," "in my power," "relaxed," "fully of energy," "moving forward." While looking at your Picture of Health, try moving or dancing around the room as if you were already in the body pictured in your drawing.

Photocopy your new drawing and put it in a place where you can see it every day.

Do this series of exercises whenever you feel physical pain or discomfort. You can use a sketchbook, plain bond paper, or sketcher's (hardbound) diary. Use paper with no lines.

PICTURE OF HEALTH

Part Two

Self-Care

Health Is an Inside Job

Health happens by design, not by accident. Good health is an inside job. No one can do it for us. Vibrant health results from knowing our needs and getting them met. It is our responsibility. These prompts will help you value yourself and your time, set priorities, and follow through. Taking good care of yourself is good for you and others. You can give more when your cup is full. So fill yours to the top.

Materials: Colored pens, markers, crayons.

Nondominant hand. Draw some images in the quadrants below, showing ways you can take better care of yourself.

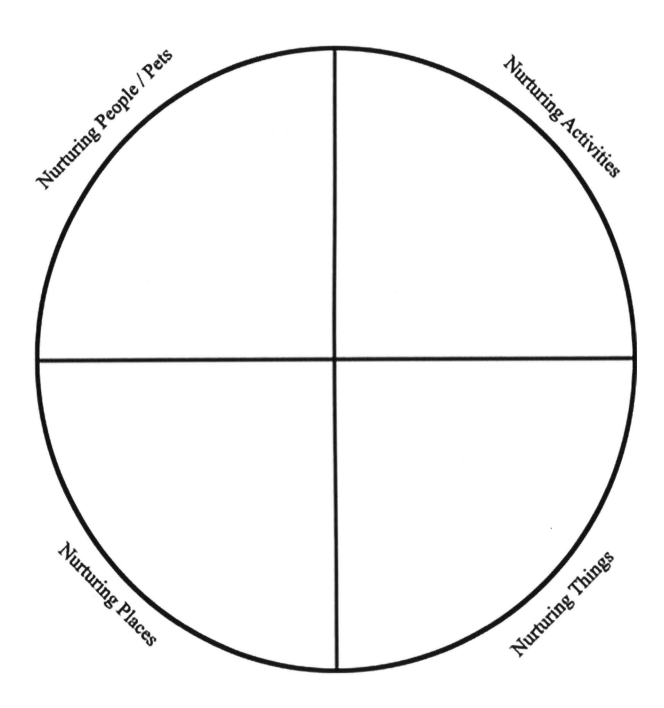

MAKING TIME FOR ME: A SELF-CARE CALENDAR

Materials: Your Taking Care of You images, colored pens, markers, crayons.

Dominant hand. In the grid below, fill in the dates for the coming month in the appropriate boxes. Select images from your Taking Care of You design. Decide when you want to include that item in your life. Draw those images into the date you chose. Coordinate this with your regular calendar or schedule.

Self-care means carving out space and time for ourselves. Saying Yes to you sometimes means saying No to others. The outside world will eat up our time if we let it. Good self-care always includes setting boundaries and limits on external demands. Sometimes external pressures are imagined or assumed. Other times they are real. Either way, it helps to identify them and to know how to tell the difference. Then we can decide what to do about them.

MAKING SPACE FOR ME

Learn to honor your own needs; picture new ways to communicate your needs to others.

Materials: Colored pens, markers, crayons.

Nondominant hand. Think of a situation in which taking better care of a specific need of yours will require setting boundaries with the outside world. Is it a person, a situation at work, home, with friends, neighbors? Pick one person or situation and draw it in box 1—Needing Boundaries, on the next page.

Dominant hand. In box 2—Setting Limits, draw a picture of yourself successfully having set limits in that situation. Show yourself feeling safe and comfortable taking care of that particular need.

NEEDING BOUNDARIES

SETTING LIMITS

SETTING BOUNDARIES

Learn to respect your needs; develop skill in setting limits on pressure from others.

Materials: Colored pens.

Dominant hand. Think of your Setting Limits picture. Write about successfully setting limits in that situation so that you could take better care of yourself. What action will you need to take?

Part Three

What's in Your Head?
Meet Your Inner Bully

Perhaps the biggest stressor is the one that lives in our own head: the Inner Bully. We all have one. It crushes our self-worth, blocks creativity, and traps us in deadening relationships and careers. The Inner Bully started in childhood with criticism from outside: name-calling, shaming, blaming. Our child-mind concluded: there must be something "wrong" with me. Then we continued bullying ourselves by repeating the insults in the first person, in our own heads: "I'm stupid, I'm ugly, I'm unlovable, or . . ." (you fill in the blanks). A pattern of negative self-talk embedded in the neuronal pathways of our brain, replaying over and over and over.

The Inner Bully tells us lies and half-truths. It says it's making things "safe" by keeping us tethered to what is familiar (even if it's making us miserable). The Inner Bully persuades us to stay in abusive relationships and unfulfilling jobs. It blocks us from following our true heart's desire. Its relentless name-calling and self-judgment can pull us down into depression, low energy, chronic anxiety, addiction, and (in extreme cases) suicidal thoughts. If we believe the Inner Bully, we remain its victim. Trying new things, growing, stretching ourselves leads us into unfamiliar territory. Our Inner Bully translates that as "unsafe" and so it resists. Fearing change, it insists that it's protecting us from harm or disappointment. It blames us for the past and shames us in advance for "mistakes" we haven't even made yet. The Inner Bully insists we be perfect or do things its way, but then condemns us for never "measuring up." We can't win.

The good news is that we can shine a spotlight on those negative thoughts inside our head and step out of the Inner Bully's shadow. You'll be doing some powerful drawing and writing processes for turning self-criticism into self-worth and positive action. Personally, I've broken through crippling writer's block with these techniques (and gone on to write twenty books). Professionally, I've witnessed hundreds of people shake off their Inner Bully and make their wildest dreams come true.

Learn to identify your Inner Bully; place your self-criticism outside yourself on the page.

Materials: Colored pens, markers, crayons (same for parts 2 and 3).

Dominant hand. On the next page, draw a picture of your Inner Bully.

WHAT MY INNER BULLY LOOKS LIKE

Unmask your Inner Bully's lies; disempower your Inner Bully by revealing what it says.

Dominant hand. Write down, **in the second person (using "you")**, the critical things you say to yourself. This is your Inner Bully talking. Write down all of its put-downs and judgments about you, your body, or any aspect of your life—e.g., **You're** *ugly*, **You're** *too fat (or too thin)*, **You'll** *never succeed in life (work, sports, etc.)*. **Note: Never say I, as in I'm stupid.** When you say or think that, you have identified with the Inner Bully and bought its put-downs. You think it is you talking. It's not—it's your Inner Bully.

WHAT MY INNER BULLY SAYS

WHAT MY INNER BULLY SAYS

49

Give vent to built-up anger at self-criticism; empower yourself to express your real feelings about self-criticism and what the Inner Bully says.

Read the Inner Bully's put-downs back to yourself. Let yourself feel the reaction in your gut that comes up when you hear what your Inner Bully says about you.

Nondominant hand. Write your answer back. Think of a bratty, mouthy kid and sass back to your Inner Bully. Get your "bratitude" on and let those feelings fly onto the page. Forget about spelling, grammar, or penmanship. Blow off some of that steam that has accumulated from years of self-put-downs, as well as put-downs from others. If three pages aren't enough, use some plain bond paper. Some people use old newspapers for this "sass back"and turn it into graffiti (four-letter words and all). After you feel finished, read aloud the "sass back" you wrote.

SASSING BACK

SASSING BACK

SASSING BACK

53

The preceding series of prompts may silence your Inner Bully for a while. But it will come back, perhaps harping on a new topic. I got the Inner Bully off my back and shed my writer's block. But the Inner Bully returns whenever I am breaking new ground: starting a new business, planning a new venture, learning a new skill. Remember, those messages got mapped into our brain wiring. But we can take back control of our thoughts whenever the Inner Bully returns. It lives in our heads, but we don't have to take anything it says personally. Decide to choose your own thoughts and actions. Don't let the Inner Bully hijack your self-worth. Choose a new, positive thought about yourself and focus on that.

TELLING THE TRUTH

Learn to tell fact from the Inner Bully's fiction; take control of your thoughts about yourself.

Materials: Colored pens, markers.

Dominant hand. Under **Inner Bully Says . . .** write out what the Inner Bully says in separate sentences. In the column **The Real Truth Is . . .**, next to each sentence your Inner Bully said, write a rebuttal stating the truth. Sentence for sentence, match wits with your Inner Bully. Example:

INNER BULLY SAYS . . .	THE REAL TRUTH IS . . .
You're not smart enough to start a successful business. You never trained in retail sales and you'll fail.	I've achieved all my major goals in life, so there's no reason to believe I won't succeed at this. My heart's in it and I work hard, getting help when I need it.

TELLING THE TRUTH

The Inner Bully Turned Outward

When we are not aware of our Inner Bully and dealing with it internally, it can easily spill over onto other people. Without our realizing it or intending to hurt others, our Inner Bully attacks others and does damage. It hurts the feelings of others and can harm or destroy relationships. Name-calling, ridiculing, and shaming others qualify as bullying. We've all had it done to us. If we are honest, we know we've also done these things to others (at one time or another).

I believe we bully others because we get sick of being beaten up by the Inner Bully, the voice of self-blaming and shaming in our own heads. We try to get that monkey off our backs by exporting it, blaming and shaming others. This is a problem in personal relationships, but is also having a far-reaching impact on our society. Bullying has reached epidemic proportions in our world. It shows up in the justice system, politics, domestic violence, and schools. Anxiety resulting from being bullied (especially cyber-bullying) is now a common cause of absenteeism and poor performance in middle and high school students in the United States. It is contributing to psychological and physical problems, self-harm, and suicide.

Bullies are covering up deep insecurity and fear. Their Inner Bully is terrorizing them. So they, in turn, terrorize others. I explained this to a high school class I was visiting in our community. "Deal with the Bully in your own head first," I told them, "then the bullies from outside won't bother you so much." They nodded knowingly and saw the truth in what I was saying. Then I taught them to answer back to their own Inner Bully. At the end of class, I received a standing ovation and students pleaded with the teacher to bring me back. These kids knew the truth when they saw it.

We can all do our part by dealing with our Inner Bully. Don't allow it to beat you up and don't let it turn outward against others. The following is an activity for dealing with our hurtful behavior toward others. This can only benefit our mental and physical health.

Learn to put the golden rule into practice; own up to how you turn your Inner Bully outward.

Materials: Colored pens, extra paper (8½ x 11 inches).

Dominant hand. Think of someone toward whom you have spoken or behaved in a hurtful, bullying way. Write a letter of apology for anything you did or said that was hurtful.

This letter is not meant for sending, but for you as an exercise in clearing your feelings and thoughts. If you wish to apologize directly to someone you've written to in private, that is your choice. You may want to write this letter out on stationery and send it. I do not advise texting an apology, as it is too impersonal.

MY LETTER OF APOLOGY

THE HEALING LETTER—2

Practice respecting yourself, your body, and your feelings.

Dominant hand. Write a letter of apology to yourself: to your body and your emotions for not always listening to them. Explain that you are learning to listen now and doing your best to take care of yourself. Thank your body for all the things it does for you. Thank your feelings for what they do for you.

APOLOGIES TO MYSELF

Part Four

With a Little Help from My Friends

The Power of Supportive Relationships

Feelings of self-worth are the foundation of all health. How you care for yourself reflects how you *feel* about yourself. Doing inner work (tending to your body, emotions, and thoughts) is an essential part of a healthy lifestyle. Hopefully, by following the prompts in parts 1 and 2, self-care has become a top priority in your life. However, our inner life must be balanced by a healthy outer life. Creating a strong network of love and support with others is essential for a healthy lifestyle.

As an art therapist I treat clients with high levels of stress and anxiety. Much of this is caused by feelings of isolation, loneliness, and even resentment. Disconnection from others is not healthy, and it is especially devastating when one is facing illness or personal crisis. While my clients are doing inner healing and learning self-care, I help them cultivate a personal support system. We identify those with whom they have a mutually nourishing relationship and acknowledge the value of those people in their lives. If an individual does not have such a support system, I help them create one as soon as possible. It makes all the difference in the world. It is also important to recognize those people with whom you are in conflict, as you did in part 2 with boundary setting in Making Space for Me and Setting Boundaries.

The great enemy of supportive relationships is the judgmental mind. When our minds are filled with destructive thoughts and beliefs, toward ourselves (the Inner Bully) or others, it becomes an enemy of our emotions, our bodies, and our relationships. Hopefully you have been cultivating self-care and are now able to connect with others from a place of less judgment (of yourself and of them). This section will strengthen your ability to reach out to others, to feel and express your appreciation for them. This is how you build a healthy support network: giving to others from a fuller cup and receiving from them in return. It is my hope that cultivating loving care for yourself enables you to give love more openly and deeply to others. That's what we all need right now.

63

The Power of Support Groups

There is something immensely empowering about coming out of isolation and sharing our private struggles with others who have walked the same path. Lending an open ear and an open heart and embracing our common humanity is an ennobling experience. It is a gift we give both to ourselves and to others.

Whether the focus is fighting cancer, recovering from drug abuse, or achieving our career goals, the power of peer support groups has been proven again and again. We have seen this documented in numerous grassroots movements. The personal growth and consciousness-raising groups of the seventies formed the foundation of the women's movement. The eighties saw a great increase in the popularity of support groups dealing with addictions, life-threatening illness, and career challenges. Twelve-step programs, such as Alcoholics Anonymous, are other examples of tried and true support group models.

You may want to consider joining a group or starting your own. If you join a group that already exists, look for one with common interests or goals and a safe, supportive atmosphere. "Safe" means that everyone contributes, no one personality dominates, there is no judgment or criticism, and clear ground rules are in place to make it a productive and mutually supportive experience for all. Depending on the nature of the group, confidentiality may need to be one of the ground rules. Twelve-step programs are a good model for support groups: "no cross-talk" when someone has the floor, confidentiality ("What is said here, stays here"), and mutually agreed-upon ground rules for keeping the group on course according to its purpose ("principles before personalities").

Cultivate appreciation and thanks for the friendships and other loving relationships that bless your life; express gratitude to help love grow and blossom within yourself and in your world.

Materials: Colored pens, markers, crayons (same materials for parts 2 and 3).

Dominant hand. In the space below, write down the names of your close friends and loved ones at this time in your life. Visualize each person as you write his or her name.

Nondominant hand. Draw a picture of you and one person from your list on the previous page. Show the nature of your relationship at this time.

Dominant hand. Write a letter to the person in your picture. Share your thoughts and feelings about how you value your relationship. You might want to copy the letter and send it, or not. Whatever feels right to you.

MY SUPPORT SYSTEM

Create an inventory of personal needs, resources, and support.

Materials: Colored pens, markers, crayons.

Who are the people you turn to when you need understanding, honest feedback, encouragement, support, or assistance of any kind? This might include family members, friends, neighbors, co-workers, and professionals who provide special services. Consider these people as your personal support system. Picture them in your mind's eye and experience the feelings you have about them. Contemplate how each of these people contributes to your life. Also picture the ways in which you support them.

On the next page, draw a large circle for you to create a diagram of your support system (like the one shown below).

Nondominant hand. Draw a picture of yourself in the center circle.

Dominant hand. Draw radial lines coming out from the center. Each line will have a name of one of your support system members. Put the person's name on the top of the line.

Dominant hand. Beneath each name (underneath the line), write a phrase that describes how that person supports you.

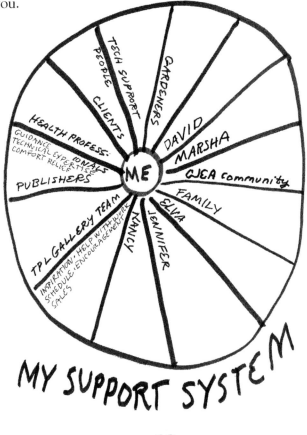

SUPPORT SYSTEM DIAGRAM—1

Dominant hand. Examine your Support System Diagram. If you feel a need to strengthen your support system, in the space below write down any changes you want to make. Implement these in your everyday life. If your assessment shows that you depend too much on one or two individuals, you may decide to broaden your base of support. Reaching out for assistance when you need it can be extremely empowering. It helps you nourish yourself and build bridges between yourself and others. It is also essential that these relationships be mutual, giving and receiving.

CHANGES I WANT TO MAKE

GRATITUDE RULES

Identify your support system members; express appreciation to those who support you.

Materials: Colored pens, extra paper (8½ x 11 inches).

Review the people in your personal support system from the previous activity. These are people you turn to when you need help and encouragement, a sounding board, information, or a different perspective on things. As you review your list, ask yourself about the *quality* of support each person provides. Are they there for you when you need them? Are you there for them? Can you count on them in a crisis? Do they accept you and allow you to be yourself?

Dominant hand. Write a note of thanks to each of the people in your support system. Thank them for their friendship, love, and support. In your note, tell each person specifically what he or she has done for you and how it has affected your life. You will need extra paper for these thank-you notes. You may feel like sending these notes or expressing your gratitude in person or via email. It's up to you.

RAINBOW HEART MEDITATION

Create your own personal support system; express gratitude to those who support you; experience yourself being loved and supported.

Materials: Colored pens, markers, crayons.

Imagine that you have invited the members of your personal support system to join you in a circle. They may be family members, friends, loved ones, pets, neighbors, coworkers, and supportive professionals. As you look around the circle, notice each one clearly. See the expressions of love and support on their faces.

Imagine a laser beam of golden light emanating from your heart and the hearts of all the people in the circle coming together in the center of the circle. These laser beams form a pool of healing energy from which a fountain of rainbows rises high into the sky. As the rainbows arc back down to earth, each one returns to a person in the circle, bringing with it the qualities of all the colors of the rainbow.

Now, meditate on the colors of the rainbow. First is the color red. Second is the color orange. Third is the color yellow. Fourth is the color green. Fifth is the color blue. The sixth color is indigo (deep violet-blue). The seventh and final ray is violet. See each person surrounded by golden light, which contains all the colors of the rainbow and brings spiritual regeneration.

Nondominant hand. Draw a picture of your Rainbow Heart Meditation on the next page. Let it be as free and fanciful as you wish. What would your ideal support group look like? (It does not have to be a formal group but can be an informal circle of friends.)

RAINBOW HEART MEDITATION

73

Centering through Mandala-Making

The word *mandala* means magic circle in Sanskrit. The mandala is a circular design radiating from a center and contained within a boundary. Mandalas occur in nature—the iris of the eye and flowers, like the daisy—and in the art and architecture of all peoples. Tibetan sand mandalas and cloth meditation banners (tankas), Native American sand paintings, and rose windows in Gothic cathedrals are mandala designs. Over the ages, mandalas have been used in measuring time and speed: the Aztec calendar stone, sundials, and more recently, clocks and speedometers. Your earlier Support System Diagrams were mandalas.

Mandalas are a wonderful focusing device for meditation and healing and a powerful tool in art therapy. Inspired by ancient art and practices, psychologist C. G. Jung was the first clinician to bring mandalas into psychotherapy as an integrative and centering device. His book *Mandala Symbolism* includes the case study of a patient who created mandalas over a period of years, showing the unfolding of the soul in vivid color and exquisite design. The mandala format is especially suited for picturing one's inner and outer worlds. Its very structure—design elements radiating out from a center point contained within a large boundary—invites you to center yourself within a larger context. For our purposes, you will use mandalas for creating your healthy lifestyle.

In addition to individual mandalas, I use group mandalas in my training programs. Each individual is given a large wedge-shaped piece to design. The pieces are then assembled to create a communal mandala showing the contribution or vision of each individual as well as the synergy of the group. It's sort of a "quilting bee" with paper. Members of the group take photos so that each member can have a record of the group mandala. Individual or group mandalas are also used in my Visioning® process using the guidelines in my book *Visioning: Ten Steps to Designing the Life of Your Dreams*.

MANDALA OF A HEALTHY LIFESTYLE

Celebrate listening to your body and emotions: design and create a healthy lifestyle.

Materials: Colored markers, pens, crayons.

Nondominant hand. On the next page, draw a large circle extending out to the edges of the page. In the center of the circle draw an image that represents you. It might be a favorite symbol (something you identify with) or a drawing or photograph of yourself.

Radiating out from that center, create a design that portrays what a healthy lifestyle looks like for you. Include images of all the important elements in your life: show the people and pets, places, activities, and things that contribute to your health.

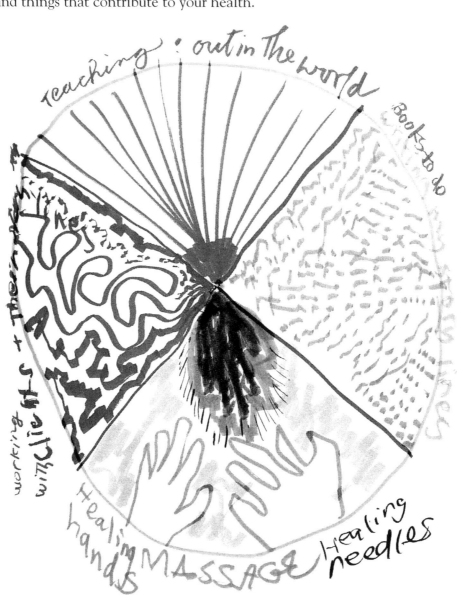

I recommend making a new mandala from time to time. Update your Mandala of a Healthy Lifestyle. It is a good idea to consult your body through written dialogue from part 1 before doing a new mandala. Ask your body what it needs: what kinds of food and exercise, rest and relaxation, relationships and work, places to live and spend time. Let your body express itself through your mandalas. Explore mixed media and larger paper. Experiment with photo collages using colored paper. Try using other drawing and painting tools (colored pencils, pastels, watercolors). Let your Inner Child and the Inner Artist come out to play.

MANDALA

79

MANDALA

81

MANDALA

To Your Health

Thank you for allowing me to guide you in listening to your body, your emotions, and your inner mental dialogue. I hope it has been helpful and rewarding. As you know, our bodies are talking to us all the time. Now you have the tools to listen deeply and find the wisdom you carry within.

This method is not intended as a substitute for medical care. Whatever else you do, please seek professional advice when you need it. The techniques in this book *are* intended to help you uncover the *emotional* aspect of illness, discomfort, acute or chronic conditions, or recovery from disease or surgery.

There is one thing I know for sure: There is *always an emotional component when the body is in pain or distress* of any kind. If you have done the prompts in this book, you have probably discovered emotions living inside your body. You may have noticed that, regardless of the cause or the length of time you have had a pain or ailment, emotions have surfaced.

In any event, feelings will always come up. That's life. Some emotions will feel comfortable, others will be more difficult. And there are some we'd rather avoid altogether. If you stop and listen to your very own self, I am confident you will discover valuable insights and guidance from your body and emotions. The inner wisdom you find becomes your trusted guide, telling you what needs healing and what you can do for yourself. This can only help you toward better health. If you are receiving medical care, you will become a proactive patient. As the old saying goes, *God helps those who help themselves*. If you do not need professional medical care, you can use these tools for self-care and prevention of illness. Either way, you empower yourself to take charge of your own health. Enjoy!

Recommended Reading & Listening

Abaci, Peter. *Conquer Your Chronic Pain: A Life-Changing Drug-Free Approach for Relief, Recovery, and Restoration*. Wayne, NJ: New Page Books, 2016.

Capacchione, Lucia. *Visioning: Ten Steps to Designing the Life of Your Dreams*. New York: Tarcher/Putnam, 2000.

————. *The Power of Your Other Hand: A Course in Channeling the Inner Wisdom of the Right Brain*. Wayne, NJ: Career Press, 2001.

————. *The Art of Emotional Healing*. Boston, MA: Shambhala, 2006.

————. *The Picture of Health* (Audio/CD). Cambria, CA: luciac.com, 2006.

————. *The Creative Journal: The Art of Finding Yourself (35th Anniversary Edition)*. Athens, OH: Swallow Press/Ohio University Press, 2015.

————. *Drawing Your Stress Away: A Do-It-Yourself Coloring Book*. Athens, OH: Swallow Press/Ohio University Press, 2017.

Chapman, Linda. *Neurobiologically Informed Trauma Therapy with Children and Adolescents: Understanding Mechanisms of Change*. New York: Norton, 2014.

Cooper, Jessie Allen. *The Sound of Feelings Sampler* (Audio/CD). Everett, WA: Cooper Sound Waves, 2007 (available at luciac.com).

Gopalan, Radha. *Second Opinion: How to Combine Eastern and Western Medical Philosophies to Increase Your Wellness and Healing Power*. Scottsdale, AZ: Plata Publishing, 2015.

Nakazawa, Donna Jackson. *Childhood Disrupted: How Your Biography Becomes Your Biology, and How You Can Heal* (New York: Simon & Schuster, 2015).

Pennebaker, James W. *Opening Up: The Healing Power of Confiding in Others*. New York: Avon Books, 1990.

————. *Writing to Heal: A Guided Journal for Recovery from Trauma and Emotional Upheaval*. Oakland, CA: New Harbinger, 2004.

Pert, Candace B. *Molecules of Emotion: Why You Feel the Way You Feel*. New York, NY: Scribner, 1997.

————. *Everything You Need to Know to Feel Go(o)d*. Carson, CA: Hay House, 2006.

Sarno, John E. *The Mindbody Prescription: Healing the Body, Healing the Pain*. New York: Warner Books, 1998.

Siegel, Daniel J. *Mindsight: The New Science of Transformation*. New York: Norton, 2010.

van der Kolk, Bessel A. *The Body Keeps the Score: Brain, Mind, and Body in the Healing of Trauma*. New York: Viking, 2014.

Body Diagrams

Feel free to photocopy the following body maps for use with this book.

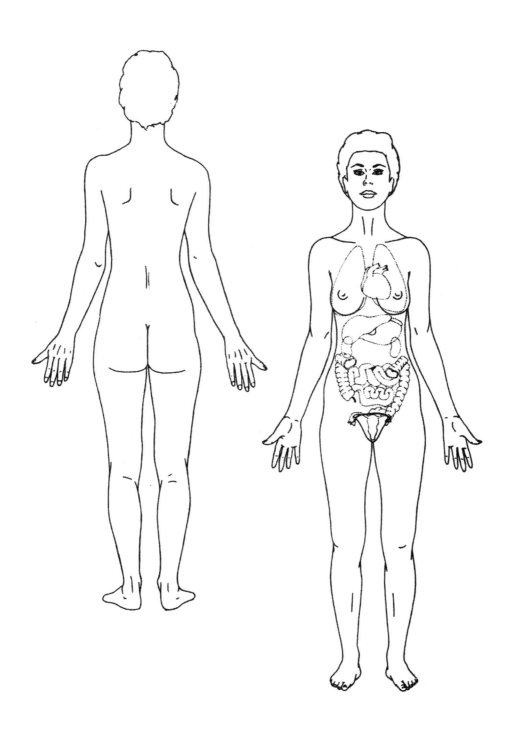

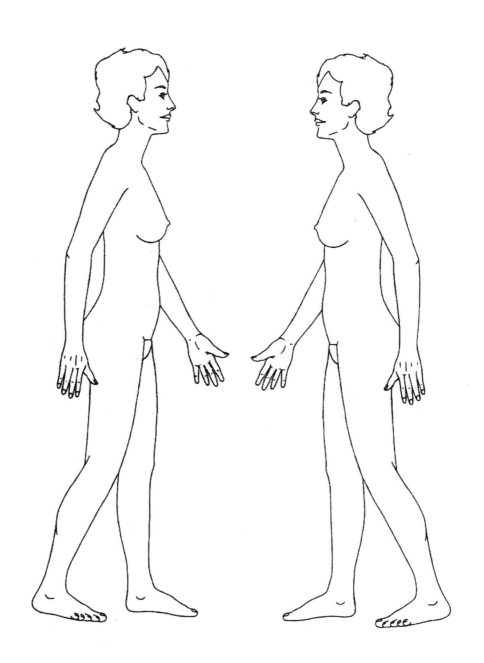

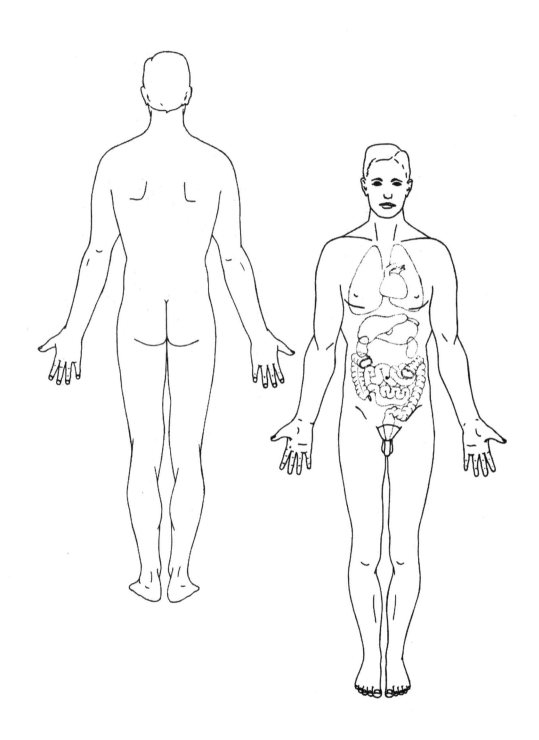

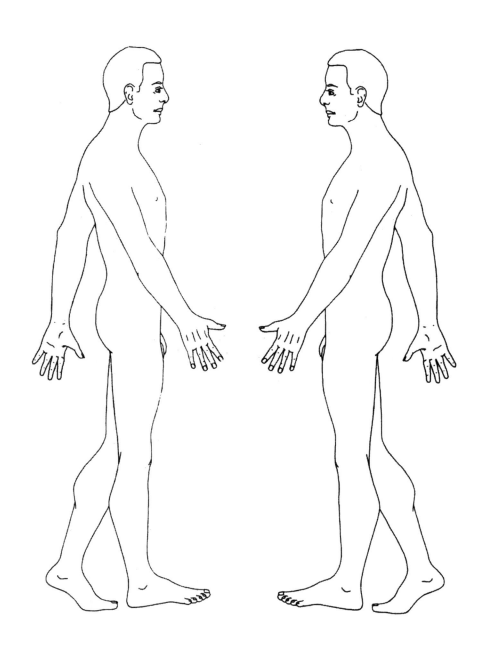